FOOD for KIDS

FOOD for KIDS

DELICIOUS, NUTRITIOUS RECIPES FOR CHILDREN

RANO SURI

Photographs: Brother's Art
Food Styling: Veenu Arya
ISBN 81-86685-07-3

Published by
Wisdom Tree
4779/23 Ansari Road
Darya Ganj, New Delhi-110002
Ph.: 23247966/67/68

Printed at
Print Perfect
New Delhi 110 0 64

INTRODUCTION

"My mummy cooks yummy!". You would love to hear this from your little one because pleasing the joy of your life is no easy matter, especially when the child seems to enjoy all that is not good for health and hates everything nutritious that you want to be eaten. How to make nutritious yet delicious food is probably the greatest challenge you face.

According to Indian culture food affects the way we think, more so is the case with children who are growing up. It is important to give them a balanced diet. This does not imply that all meals should be balanced; rather all meals every day should add up to a balance. If they have had a hot pizza for lunch (with all the *maida* in it) then they can be given a tangy fruit salad in the evening. Actually even the pizza can be made nutritious by adding mushrooms, capsicums, *paneer,* etc. Your child may not take to your latest experiment with food (try to recall your experience when you were a child and your father insisted on your eating his own variation of *badam kheer*!) , but the child of today is certainly far more adventurous. So don't lose heart! Try the same recipe again after a few days but this time in combination with his or her favourite dish. It does not take much for children to change their minds and what they hated last week might in no time at all become their favourite! Another excellent way of trying new recipes is to pack them for school-lunch or serve them when your child's friends come over to your house. Eating while having fun with friends is probably the best way to enjoy food. Also, on finding the friends appreciating your food (remember, we all still like our friend's home-cooked food, because the same *moong dal* tastes so delicious and different when cooked in your friends's home), your child would not only feel proud of you but would love to try out his mummy's new recipes (and, relish too) !

CONTENTS

THE PERFECT START

A PORTABLE FEAST

MOUTHMELTING QUICKIES

SENSATIONAL SOUPS

BLOCKBUSTERS

SWEET TREAT AND SHAKES

THE PERFECT START

A big smile and a relaxed and delicious breakfast is just the perfect start to the day for your child. As they are charged with energy early in the morning and are brimming with life it's a good idea to give them a light but nutritious breakfast after they have got over their physical exercise. Let the sun shine and your culinary skills bring joy on their lovely faces!

BREAD CRISPERS (CANOPIES)

Serve 6 persons • Preparation time 20 minutes • Baking time 10 minutes + 5 minutes

Ingredients for canopies
6 fresh bread slices
butter as desired (about 6 tsp)
a pinch each of salt and pepper

Ingredients for filling
2 medium-size boiled potatoes chopped into small pieces
½ cup boiled peas
1 finely chopped capsicum
1 finely chopped tomato
1 finely diced carrot
½ tsp salt
¼ tsp pepper
4 tsp chopped coriander leaves
4-5 tsp cream
2 grated cheese cubes
4-5 tsp tomato ketchup

- Spread butter lightly on all the slices.
- Grease the aluminium or steel bowls *(katoris)*.
- Press one slice in each *katori* so that it acquires the same shape as that of the *katori*.
- Trim the extra portions.
- Repeat the process for all the slices.
- Pre-heat the oven at 200°C for 8 to 10 minutes and bake the canapes till brown and crisp.
- Loosen the sides and take out the canopies.

Method for filling

- Mix all the ingredients given for the filling with exception of

....continued

ketchup, in a bowl.

- Fill the bread canopies with the filling and add a dash of ketchup on top of each.
- Bake them again for 5 minutes.
- Serve on a bed of cabbage and with potato wafers.

Try This Variation

The filling can be varied to suit individual tastes. Instead of potatoes use 200 gms *paneer* (cut into cubes), boiled mushrooms (200 gms) or 6 boiled eggs chopped into cubes.

HARA-BHARA PARANTHA

Serve 4 persons • Preparation time 30 minutes • Cooking time 20 minutes

Ingredients

1 cup whole wheat flour (*atta*)
1 cup flour (*maida*)
1 cup spinach puree (100 gms spinach leaves chopped, churned with a little water)
2 tsp butter or *ghee*
1 level tsp salt
½ tsp caraway seeds (*ajwain*)
a little lukewarm water for kneading the dough

Ingredients for filling

1 cup *paneer*
1 finely chopped onion
½ cup chopped coriander leaves
2 chopped green chillies
a few chopped mint leaves
salt to taste
½ tsp roasted cumin seeds (ground *jeera*)
3 or 4 tsp thick cream or *malai*

- Sieve flour, *maida* and salt together.
- Add butter or melted *ghee, ajwain*, and spinach puree.
- Mix thoroughly.
- Add water as required to make a soft and smooth dough.
- Cover it with a wet napkin and keep aside for half an hour.
- Grate *paneer*, add the chopped onions, green chillies, coriander leaves, chopped mint leaves, salt and roasted ground ***jeera*** and thick cream.
- Mix till the mixture becomes smooth.
- Take the dough and divide it into 8 equal portions to make round balls.
- Roll 2 equal size *chapatis.*

continued...

- Spread $1/4$ of the filling evenly on 1 *chapati.*
- Place the second *chapati* on top of it.
- Seal the edges by pressing and lightly roll it.
- Now cook the *parantha* on a pre-heated and greased *tava*.
- It should be fried with melted *ghee* applied on both sides till crisp.
- Serve with beaten curd.

GRILLED BURGERS

Serve 4 persons • Preparation time 15 minutes • Baking time 20 minutes

Ingredients
2 burger buns or hotdog buns
butter as desired
2 boiled and mashed potatoes
4 tsp tomato ketchup
a few onion rings
1 chopped capsicum
½ cup boiled macaroni or 4 to 5 boiled mushrooms
a pinch each of salt and pepper
2 cheese cubes
chopped coriander leaves

- Cut the buns horizontally into 2 halves.
- Spread a little butter on each piece.
- Add a pinch of salt and pepper to the mashed potatoes and spread a thin layer on each piece.
- Spread 1 tsp ketchup over each potato layer.
- Top this with rings of onion, bits of capsicum and boiled macaroni or mushrooms.
- Sprinkle a pinch of salt and pepper over each piece.
- Add grated cheese on top. Pre-heat the oven to 200°C.
- Place open burgers in the middle shelf for 6 to 7 minutes and bake till crisp.
- Garnish with coriander leaves.

continued...

Add a drop of ketchup in the centre.

Try This Variation

The topping can be grated boiled egg, chopped tomatoes, shredded cabbage rolled in thick cream. Instead of buns *kulchas* can be used.

PANEER CREAM ROLLS

Serve 6 persons • Preparation time 30 minutes • Cooking time 15 minutes

Ingredients
400 gms *paneer*
1 big grated potato
salt to taste
½ tsp black or white pepper
1/3 tsp mustard powder
1 cup fresh bread crumbs
(4 bread slices churned in a grinder or mixer)
1/3 cup , lightly beaten cream or fresh *malai*
flour (*maida*) for coating
oil for frying

- Grate the *paneer* and potato.
- Add salt, pepper and mustard powder.
- Add fresh bread crumbs.
- Mix all the ingredients and mash them till smooth.
- Now take a small portion of the mixture and make oval-shaped rolls, approximately 2" long and 1" in diameter.
- Make a deep hole with a fingertip in each roll and fill 1 tsp cream inside (you can use the piping bag).
- Seal the edges of the roll, coat with *maida* and dust it.
- Make all the *paneer* rolls in a similar manner.
- Fry the rolls in hot oil, till golden brown.
- Serve these on a bed of cabbage and cucumber salad.

....continued

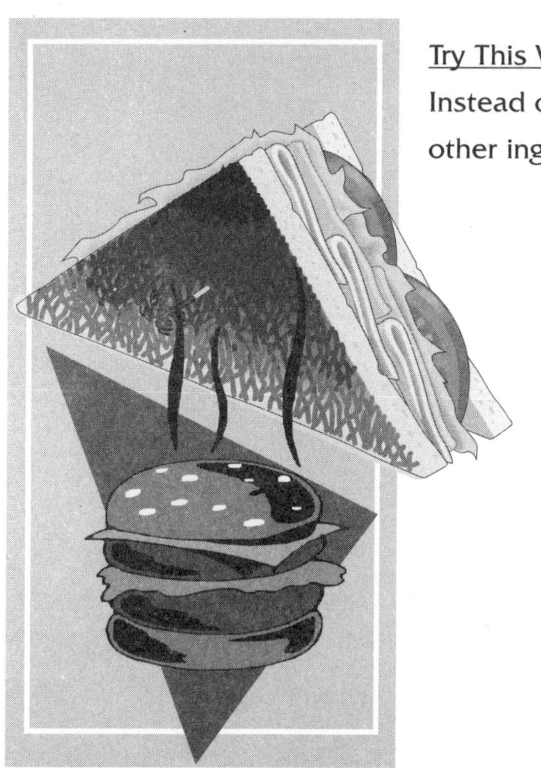

Try This Variation

Instead of *paneer*, ½ kg boiled potatoes can be used. All the other ingredients remain the same.

FLUFFY TOAST

Serve 4 persons • Preparation time 15 minutes • Baking Time 5 minutes

Ingredients
4 bread slices
butter to taste
4 eggs
salt and pepper to taste
chopped coriander leaves
2 grated cheese cubes

- Spread butter lightly on bread slices.
- Separate egg-yolks and egg-whites.
- Leave the egg-yolk in egg-shell.
- Beat the whites of eggs till soft and fluffy (till peaks are formed).
- Pile the bread slices with whites of eggs and place the egg-yolk in centre.
- Sprinkle salt and pepper.
- Sprinkle grated cheese and garnish with coriander leaves.
- Bake the bread with fluffy eggs in a pre-heated oven at 200°C for 5 minutes till golden brown.
- Serve hot with ketchup.

CREAMY VEGGIE SANDWICH

Serve 6 persons • Preparation time 15 minutes • Cooking time 15 minutes

Ingredients
1 cup finely shredded cabbage
1 cup thickly grated carrot
1 boiled and grated potato
1 grated cheese cube
1 cup white sauce
½ cup cream
1 tsp salt
½ tsp white or black pepper
1/3 tsp mustard powder
½ tsp castor sugar (ground sugar)
6 bread slices or as desired
butter as required

Ingredients for white sauce
2 tsp butter
2 tsp flour (*maida*)
1 cup milk
6 tsp water

- Mix together white sauce, cream, salt, pepper mustard powder and sugar till smooth.
- Add cabbage, carrot, grated and boiled potato and grated cheese. Mix thoroughly.
- Remove the hard crust of bread slices and spread a thin layer of butter.
- Spread the mixture (2 or 3 tsp) on one buttered slice and arrange the second slice on it.
- Cut it into two sandwiches.
- Garnish with shredded lettuce leaves and grated carrots.
- Cover these with aluminium foil or wet napkin.
- Keep in the refrigerator for ½ an hour.

continued...

- Serve with tomato ketchup.

WHITE SAUCE

- Melt butter and add flour (sifted).
- Cook on slow fire for 2 minutes.
- Remove from fire and add milk, stirring continuously till smooth.
- Cook on slow fire till the mixture is thick like fresh custard.
- You can add 4 tsp of cheese spread instead of grated cheese cube.

CARROT PARANTHA

Serve 6 persons • Preparation time 15 minutes • Cooking time 25 minutes

Ingredients
for outer covering (dough)
2 cups whole wheat flour (*atta*)
2 cups flour (*maida*)
1 tsp salt
4 tsp butter or *desi ghee* (clarified butter)
½ tsp *ajwain*
a little lukewarm milk for kneading the dough

Ingredients for filling
6-8 thickly grated carrots
1 boiled and grated potato
1 finely chopped onion
1 tsp butter
2 finely chopped green chillies
chopped coriander leaves
a few mint leaves
1 tsp lemon juice
oil or *ghee* for cooking

- Sieve *atta, maida* and salt together.
- Add butter and *ajwain.*
- Mix thoroughly.
- Add lukewarm milk and make a smooth, soft dough.

FILLING

- Melt butter, cook onion, green chillies, coriander leaves and mint leaves in it for 2 minutes on a high flame.
- Add carrots and cook for a minute.
- Remove this from fire and add lemon juice.
- Cool the filling.
- Make two medium size balls and roll them into a *chappati*.

continued...

- Spread 6 tsp of filling on one rolled *chappati* and arrange the second *chappati* on it.
- Seal the edges by pressing and lightly roll it.
- Now heat the girdle (*tava*) and grease it.
- Fry the carrot-stuffed *parantha* on it by adding oil or *ghee*.
- Cook till the *parantha* is golden brown on both sides.
- Serve hot with beaten curd or potato *raita.*

Fluffy Toast ➢
Overleaf Malaysian Envelope

A PORTABLE FEAST

It is absolutely important for your child to have a healthy, nutritious lunch but it should not be so sumptuous that his or her concentration level drops after the lunch-break in school. Sandwiches may constitute an integral part of the tiffin but make sure to avoid fillings which will make the bread go soggy. Baked food as also stuffed ***parantha*** and fresh fruits are good for the child's lunch-box. It is essential that lunch-boxes are kept clean and tidy to prevent bacterial or fungal growth. Empty out bits of left-over food and wash the box daily; dry it thoroughly before storing, leaving the lid off. It is advisable to keep a spare tiffin-box at home which can come handy in case your child forgets his own in school.

Ingredients
4 hard boiled eggs
4 or 5 tsp butter
salt to taste
¼ tsp black or white pepper
1 grated cheese cube (optional)
chopped coriander leaves
12 bread slices
butter as desired

EGG SANDWICH

Serve 6 persons • Preparation time 20 minutes

- Shell the eggs and mash them.
- Add salt, pepper and butter. Mix thoroughly till smooth.
- Add cheese and coriander leaves. Keep aside.
- Remove the hard crust from the bread slices and butter them.
- Spread 2 tsp of egg mixture between 2 slices and press them. Cut into 2 triangular pieces.
- Arrange the sandwiches on a bed of cabbage or lettuce leaves. Serve with cucumber and tomato salad.

Try This Variation

Instead of 4 eggs, 250 gms *paneer* (cottage cheese) can be used.

VERMICELLI PULAO

Serve 4 persons • Cooking time 8 to 10 minutes • Preparation time 10 minutes

Ingredients

1 packet of vermicelli
2 or 3 tsp clarified butter (*desi ghee*)
½ tsp cumin seeds (*jeera*)
2 or 3 crushed cardamoms (*elaichi*)
¼ tsp *garam masala*
1 finely chopped onion
1 diced carrot
1 small capsicum
½ cup finely cut spinach
¼ tsp sugar
salt to taste
1 tsp lemon juice

- Boil the vermicelli for a minute with ½ tsp oil and ¼ tsp salt.
- Drain and keep aside.
- In a pan heat *ghee.* Add cumin seeds and stir.
- Add onions and crushed cardamoms and cook till onions are golden in colour.
- Add *garam masala* and mix.
- Add carrot, capsicum and spinach.
- Cook for 2 minutes on high flame and add the boiled vermicelli, salt and sugar.
- Mix well and cook again on high flame for 3 to 4 minutes.
- Sprinkle lemon juice and garnish with coriander leaves.
- Serve plain or with onion *raita.*

TIP Home-made vermicelli can also be used instead of long vermicelli as it looks more appetising and resembles rice.

SPINACH SQUARES

Preparation time 10 minutes + 20 minutes standing time • Cooking time 10 minutes

Ingredients
½ cup semolina (*sooji*)
1 cup pressed flour (*maida*)
½ tsp salt
½ tsp baking powder
¼ tsp crushed garlic
4 tsp butter
¼ tsb roasted and coarsely ground coriander powder
½ cup spinach puree
1 grated cheese cube

- Sieve *maida, sooji,* salt and baking powder together.
- Add butter and mix with fingertips till it resembles bread crumbs. Mix garlic, cumin powder and grated cheese.
- Add spinach puree and knead the dough till smooth but not very soft. Cover and keep aside for 20 minutes.
- Roll one-third of the dough with a rolling pin.
- Cut this into squares (2").
- Prick each square with a fork and dust with a little flour. Keep aside for 5 minutes. Repeat with the remaining dough.
- Deep fry in hot oil till golden brown.
- Serve with tomato ketchup or garlic chilli sauce.
- This can be stored in air-tight boxes after cooling.

Ingredients

1 packet (200 gms) boiled macaroni
2 tbsp refined oil
2 finely chopped garlic flakes
2 spring onions, chopped with some green leafy portion or 2 medium-sized chopped onions
1 diced big carrot
1 finely chopped capsicum
100 gms mushrooms, chopped into thin pieces
½ tsp red chilli powder
1 cup fresh tomato puree (4 chopped and churned tomatoes)
salt to taste
½ tsp sugar
1 shredded cabbage (small)
a few chopped spinach leaves
1 grated cheese cube

KIDDY MACARONI

Serve 4 persons • Preparation time 15 minutes • Cooking time 15 minutes

- Heat oil, add garlic and stir.
- Add the onions and cook (for approx. 4 minutes) till transparent.
- Add ½ tsp red chilli powder and stir.
- Mix in the carrot, capsicum and mushroom.
- Sauté it for 3 to 4 minutes.
- Add fresh tomato puree, salt and sugar. Cook for a minute.
- Add boiled macaroni, cabbage and spinach and cook for 4 or 5 minutes. Add grated cheese on top after taking off the flame.

continued...

- Before serving sprinkle tomato ketchup. Serve plain or with garlic bread.

HOW TO BOIL MACARONI

Boil 4 cups of water along with ½ tsp oil and ½ tsp salt. Then add macaroni and cook for 5 minutes on high flame. Stir, so that it does not stick to the bottom. Keep it in the same water for 5 minutes. Pass it through a sieve and rinse with cold water.

Ingredients
1 cup flour
8 to 10 tsp butter
¼ tsp salt
½ tsp cumin seeds (*jeera*)
½ tsp baking powder
2 grated cheese cubes
oil for frying
milk as desired

CRUNCHY CURLS

Make 30 curls • Preparation time 10 minutes • Cooking time 10 minutes

- Sieve *maida* (flour), salt and baking powder together.
- Mix butter with finger tips till it resembles bread crumbs.
- Mix cumin seeds and cheese.
- Add milk little by little and knead the mixture to make a dough (as for *puris*). Keep it covered for 20 minutes.
- Now roll out one-third of the dough with a rolling pin, keeping it one-sixth inch thick.
- Cut the sides and make squares or rectangles.
- Cut these into ¼" strips.
- Dust a little flour on them. Keep aside for 5 minutes.
- Carefully roll each strip into a curl.
- Deep fry in hot oil till golden brown.
- This can be stored in an air-tight jar.

Ingredients
1 cup semolina (*sooji* or *rava*)
2 tsp butter
1 small finely chopped onion
3 or 4 finely chopped green chillies
1 cup milk
1 cup water
½ cup desicated or grated fresh coconut
4 tsp dry or fresh bread crumbs
1 tsp salt
4 tsp chopped coriander leaves
1 tsp grated ginger
1 tsp roasted cumin seeds (ground *jeera*) curry leaves nuts and raisins
flour (*maida*) for coating oil for frying

SEMOLINA HEARTS

Serve 6 persons • Preparation time 40 minutes • Cooking time 20 minutes

- Melt butter
- Add onion and green chillies. Cook for 2 to 3 minutes till the onions are transparent.
- Add semolina (*sooji*). Stir and cook on medium flame for 2 to 3 minutes.
- Gradually add milk and water.
- Cook on medium flame till thick and then refrigerate for ½ an hour till it becomes firm.
- Mix salt, coriander leaves, curry leaves, ginger, ground *jeera*, nuts, raisins, desicated coconut and bread crumbs. Mash till smooth.
- Flatten the mixture on a greased surface with a rolling pin, cut

continued...

into ½ inch thick hearts with a heart-shaped cutter.

- Coat each piece with *maida* and dust it.
- Roll out the left-over mixture, cut into small hearts and dust each with flour (*maida*) .
- Fry the semolina hearts in hot oil till golden brown.
- Serve hot with mint *chutney* prepared in curd.
- Semolina hearts can be kept in the refrigerator for 2 days. At the time of serving, fry them.

<u>Try This Variation</u>

Instead of desicated coconut and curry leaves, and 2 cheese cubes grated finely, ¼ tsp oregano can be used.

Semolina hearts can be shaped with hands by taking a little portion at a time, if the heart-shaped cutter is not available.

Ingredients
2 big or 2 medium-size boiled potatoes
½ cup boiled peas
½ tsp salt
¼ tsp white pepper
¼ tsp mustard powder
½ cup white sauce or cream
½ cup cornflakes
a few finely chopped mint leaves
12 bread slices
butter as desired

CHEESY SURPRISE

Serve 6 persons • Preparation time 20 minutes

- Grate the potatoes.
- Add peas, salt, pepper and mustard powder and mix thoroughly.
- Add white sauce (as explained earlier in Creamy Veggie Sandwich)first and then the cornflakes and mint leaves. Mix thoroughly.
- Remove the hard crust from the sides of the bread slices and butter the slices evenly.
- Spread 4 tsp of the prepared mixture between 2 bread slices.
- Press and cut these into 2 triangular pieces.
- Serve on a bed of lettuce leaves after garnishing with mint leaves, grated carrot and potato wafers.

MOUTHMELTING QUICKIES

"**Mommy, I'm hungry.....**" On returning from the playground your little one is not willing to wait even for a second. He wants something to eat immediately as he is famished. You have to keep evening snacks ready which should be nutritious as well as easy to prepare and serve. Else your child is apt to demand fast foods like wafers or biscuits which do more harm than good. It is important to serve snacks which are light but filling and which leave the child looking forward to dinner that you have cooked so lovingly for him. It's a good idea to keep nuts, dry fruits, fresh fruits, carrot sticks readily available in case preparation of snacks were to take extra time (you never can tell when your LPG cylinder will get empty, leaving you high and dry)!

Ingredients

½ kg or 6 boiled potatoes
2 grated cheese cubes
2 lightly beaten eggs
salt to taste
½tsp white or black pepper
1/3 tsp mustard powder
oil for frying

CHEESE DROPS

Serve 6 persons • Cooking time 10 minutes

- Grate boiled potatoes.
- Add grated cheese, eggs, salt, pepper and mustard powder.
- Mix the ingredients with a fork, till smooth.
- Heat the oil.
- Take a little portion of the mixture, shape into round drops and fry on medium flame till the drops are golden brown.
- Serve with cucumber salad and lettuce leaves.

Try This Variation

Eggs can be replaced with 4 or 5 tsp cornflour and ¼ tsp baking powder.

Ingredients for fingers

400 gms *paneer* (cut into ½" by 2" strips)
½ tsp salt
½ tsp black or white pepper
¼ tsp garlic paste
oil for cooking

Ingredients for batter

1 cup flour (*maida*)
2/3 tsp salt
½ tsp baking powder
¼ tsp garlic paste
water as required
2 or 3 finely chopped green chillies
chopped coriander leaves
2 grated cheese cubes

CHEESE FINGERS

Serve 4 persons • Cooking time 8 to 10 minutes

- Sieve *maida,* salt and baking powder together.
- Add garlic and pour water slowly to make a thick batter (like *pakora* batter).
- Mix the green chillies, coriander leaves and grated cheese in it (if after adding cheese you find the batter thick, add more water and mix thoroughly).
- Keep the batter aside for 20 to 30 minutes.
- Rub salt, pepper and garlic on the *paneer* fingers and keep aside for 10 to 15 minutes.
- Heat oil. Dip each *paneer* finger into the batter and fry till golden brown.
- Serve hot on shredded cabbage bed with tomato ketchup.

Try This Variation

Use bread strips in place of *paneer* fingers.

Ingredients

6 medium-size potatoes (peel, wash and pat dry with a clean napkin)
salt to taste
½ tsp red chilli powder
1 tsp coriander powder
¼ tsp garlic paste
3 tsp lemon juice or ½ tsp mango powder (*amchur*)
4 or 5 tsp gram flour (*besan*)
oil or *ghee* for frying

POTATO CRISPERS

Serve 6 persons • Preparation time 15 minutes • Cooking time 10 minutes

- Slice the potatoes into fingers.
- Rub salt, red chilli powder, coriander powder, garlic and lemon juice on them.
- Heat oil in a frying pan till smoking hot.
- At the time of frying, sieve *besan* and coat the fingers with it by sprinkling the *besan* over them.
- Fry till nicely golden brown.
- Garnish with coriander leaves and onion rings.
- Serve with a dash of lemon juice.

Ingredients
4 eggs
½ cup milk
salt and pepper to taste
1 small finely chopped onion
1 small capsicum, chopped into small bits
1 small carrot diced into small cubes
½ cup shredded cabbage
1 small tomato cut into small pieces
4 tsp butter

SCRAMBLED SURPRISE

Serve 4 persons • Preparation time 10 minutes • Cooking time 5 minutes

- Beat the eggs.
- Add milk, salt and pepper and again beat the mixture.
- Keep aside.
- Melt butter in a pan. Add the onion. Cook for 2 minutes.
- Add carrot, capsicum and cabbage and cook for 2 minutes.
- Add tomatoes and then add beaten eggs and cook on medium flame.
- Scramble the mixture while it is being cooked.
- Serve with toasted bread and butter.

Ingredients
8 bread slices
butter as desired
4 grated cheese cubes
2 big tomatoes
½ cup boiled peas or capsicum pieces
a few coriander leaves

OPEN SANDWICH

Serve 4 persons • Preparation time 20 minutes

- Cut bread slices with a round cutter or a big *katori* or glass.
- Spread butter on each slice.
- Grate ½ cheese cube on each slice.
- Cut round slices of tomatoes and remove the inner pulp, leaving the outer red circles.
- Arrange them on each slice.
- Place boiled peas or capsicum bits in the centre.
- Garnish with coriander leaves and ketchup.

Potato Boats,
Crunchy Curls ➢
Overleaf Duckling Salad

Ingredients
4 bread slices
2 boiled and grated potatoes
salt to taste
pinch of pepper
2 grated cheese cubes
chopped coriander leaves
tomato ketchup for garnishing
oil for frying

CRISPY BREAD BITES

Serve 4 persons • Preparation time 10 minutes • Cooking time 5 minutes

- Cut the bread slices into two halves and make 8 equal rectangular pieces.
- Fry the bread pieces in hot oil till golden brown.
- Mix salt and pepper in mashed potatoes and spread on the bread slices.
- Grate cheese on each slice.
- Drop ½ tsp tomato ketchup in the centre and garnish with coriander leaves.

MINTY BREAD BITES

Ingredients
4 bread slices
butter as desired
½ cup grated *paneer* (100 gms)
4 tsp mint *chutney*
½ cup crushed cornflakes
2 grated cheese cubes
1 finely chopped tomato

Serve 6 persons • Preparation time 15 minutes • Baking time 6 minutes

- Cut each bread slice lengthwise into 4 strips.
- Spread butter on each bread strip.
- Mix grated *paneer* and mint *chutney* till smooth.
- Spread a thick layer of this mixture on each bread strip.
- Grate cheese on each slice.
- Pe-heat oven at 200°C and bake the bread strips till they become crisp and the cheese melts.
- Serve on a bed of cabbage and garnish with bits of tomato or ketchup.

Ingredients
4 *kulchas* (leavened bread)
butter as required
300 gms crumbled *paneer*
1 finely chopped onion
1 or 2 green chillies or 1 small capsicum
a few chopped coriander leaves
2 tomatoes chopped into small pieces
a few nuts and raisins
2 tsp cream
salt to taste
100 gms mozzarella cheese

KULCHA CRISPERS

Serve 4 persons • Preparation time 10 minutes • Baking time 10 minutes

- Spread a thin layer of butter on the *kulchas.*
- In a bowl mix *paneer,* onion, green chilli, coriander leaves, chopped tomatoes, nuts, raisins and salt together.
- Add cream and mix again.
- Spread the above mixture on *kulchas.* and on top of the mixture spread a layer of grated cheese.
- Bake in a pre-heated oven at 200° C for 10 minutes, till crisp.
- Serve hot and sprinkle tomato ketchup on top.

SESAME BREAD CREPES

Serve 2 persons • Preparation time 5 minutes • Cooking time 4 minutes

Ingredients
2 large bread slices
1 thickly sliced tomato
2 cheese singles (slices)
1 big, lightly beaten egg
pinch of salt and pepper
sesame seeds
butter as desired
oil for shallow frying

- Lightly spread butter on the bread slices.
- Arrange 1 cheese slice on a bread slice, then tomato slices and the second cheese slice.
- Cover this with the second bread slice and press.
- Now lightly beat the egg and add a pinch of salt and pepper.
- Dip the prepared bread sandwich in egg and coat it with sesame seeds.
- Shallow fry in hot oil till nicely golden brown.
- Cut into pieces and serve on a cabbage bed with tomato ketchup and cheese sauce.

PARSI KEBAB

Serve 6 persons • Preparation time 20 minutes • Cooking time 10 minutes

Ingredients
4 big boiled potatoes
1 cup *channa dal* (soak for 15 minutes, then boil with ½ tsp salt and 1 cup water, pressure cook after whistle at high flame for 5 minutes)
salt to taste
5 or 6 green chillies chopped
coriander leaves chopped
½ tsp grated garlic
2 tsp grated ginger
1 tsp ground *zeera*
2/3 cup desicated coconut powder
1 small chopped onion
1 tsp *amchur* or 3 tsp lemon juice
4 bread slices
few nuts and raisins
maida for coating
oil for frying
shredded cheese

- Grate potatoes.
- Put two-third of the dal in the potatoes and mix it.
- Add 3 green chillies, a few coriander leaves, 1/3 cup coconut powder, salt, *zeera, amchur,* onion, ginger, garlic, crushed bread slices without sides and cheese to the mixture.
- Mix it till smooth like *atta.*
- Make 10 balls and press them slightly with your fingers.

FILLING

- To the 1/3 cup dal, add 3 green chillies, a few coriander leaves, salt, 1/3 cup coconut powder, raisins and nuts.
- Mix it with wet hands.
- Place equal amounts of filling inside the 10 pieces of potato mixture.
- Seal and give it a desired shape.
- Coat with *maida* and fry.
- Serve with onion rings and *pudina* chutney.

SENSATIONAL SOUPS

" I don't like to eat this vegetable ...!" Vegetables that your child abhors but which are the single most important source of minerals and vitamins, can be given by cooking them in soup form. The taste of vegetables like spinach, beetroot, gourd, etc. can be camouflaged very subtly this way. Other ingredients and spices can be added to impart flavour to the soup. These attractive appetizers and lip-smacking recipes will be enjoyed not only by your children but you and your friends too.

TOMATO AND RICE SOUP

Serve 4 persons • Preparation time 15 minutes • Cooking time 15 minutes

Ingredients
½ kg finely diced tomatoes
1 cinnamon stick (*dalchini*)
2 cloves
2 chopped garlic flakes
½ boiled rice
3 cups water
salt to taste (1 tsp)
¼ tsp pepper
1 tsp sugar
2 basil (*tulsi*) leaves
3 tsp cornflour
½ cup water for mixing cornflour
6 tsp cream
a few mint leaves
2 bread slices for making croutons

- Cook the tomatoes, cinnamon, cloves, garlic in water for 5 to 6 minutes.
- Cool and churn it till the puree is smooth. If desired you can pass it through a sieve and remove the pulp.
- Add 3 cups of water and cook to boil.
- Add salt, pepper and sugar and cook for 2 more minutes.
- Mix 3 tsp cornflour with ½ cup water and add to soup.
- Add rice and chopped basil leaves.
- Simmer for 2 minutes and add cream, cook for another 2 minutes. Remove from flame.
- Serve with croutons and mint leaves.

LEMON AND SPINACH SOUP

Serve 6 persons • Preparation time 6 minutes • Cooking time 20 minutes

Ingredients
200 gms spinach
½ tsp salt
2 cloves
2 garlic flakes
½ cup water
3 tsp butter
1 small finely chopped onion
3 tsp flour (*maida*)
5 cups of water
1 tsp salt
½ tsp sugar
2 tsp cornflour
½ cup cream
2 tsp tomato ketchup
3 tsp lemon juice
bread croutons as desired

- Remove the stems of the spinach leaves. Wash them and thickly chop them.
- Boil spinach leaves along with salt, cloves, garlic and water for 5 minutes on a high flame.
- Cool the mixture and make a puree.
- In a separate pan melt butter, add onion and cook till transparent.
- Add 3 tsp flour (sifted). Stir well.
- Remove from fire.
- Add spinach puree and stir continuously till smooth.
- Mix together 5 cups of water, lemon juice and spinach soup, pouring one ingredient at a time.
- Cook on a high flame for 4 to 5 minutes.
- Add salt and sugar.

continued...

- In a separate bowl mix cornflour with a little water and pour into the soup.
- Cook this on slow fire for 3 to 4 minutes.
- Add lemon juice and cream and cook again for 2 minutes.
- Pour soup in bowls.
- Add croutons.
- Garnish with cream and tomato ketchup.

CORN AND VEGETABLE SOUP

Serve 6 persons • Preparation time 10 minutes • Cooking time 15 minutes

Ingredients

1 cup boiled corn or ½ tin of whole sweet corn (kernels)
3-4 chopped french beans
1 small diced carrot
3 or 4 chopped mushrooms
1 small floret of cauliflower chopped into bits
4 or 5 chopped spinach leaves
1 small spring onion (only green part)
6 cups of water
1 tsp salt
1/3 tsp white or black pepper
4 tsp cornflour
½ cup water for mixing cornflour
1 tsp lemon juice

- Add salt to the water and boil.
- Add corns, beans, carrots, mushrooms and cauliflower and boil for 4 minutes on a high flame.
- Add the spring onions and spinach.
- Cook for a minute.
- Add pepper.
- Mix 4 tsp cornflour with half cup water and add to the soup.
- Cook on slow fire till the soup thickens slightly.
- Add 1 tsp lemon juice and serve with soup sticks or dinner rolls.

Ingredients

2 medium-size peeled and chopped beetroot
4 chopped tomatoes
2 cloves
1 cinnamon stick
2 garlic flakes
1 cup water
2 small pieces of bread slices
1 bowl finely chopped vegetables (cabbage, carrot, beans and cauliflower, etc.)
1 cup boiled noodles
4 cups of water
1 tsp salt
½ tsp pepper

VEGETABLE AND BEETROOT SOUP

Serve 6 persons • Preparation time 5 minutes • Cooking time 15 minutes

- Put chopped beetroot, tomatoes, cloves, cinnamon, garlic and the small pieces of bread in a pressure cooker.
- Add a cup of water and pressure cook for 5 minutes on a high flame.
- Cool and churn the pulp till smooth.
- Pass it through a sieve.
- Add 4 cups of water and 1 tsp salt.
- Cook till it boils.
- Add chopped vegetables and cook further for 5 minutes on high flame.
- Add boiled noodles and pepper and cook for another minute.
- Serve with soup sticks, dinner rolls and butter.

Ingredients
100 gms soaked and peeled almonds(approx. 1 cup)
1 finely chopped small onion
3 tsp butter
3 tsp flour (*maida*)
1 cup milk
4 cups water
1 tsp salt
½ tsp pepper
½ cup cream
a pinch of sugar

ALMOND SOUP

Serve 4 persons • Preparation time 10 minutes • Cooking time 15 minutes

- Chop 20 almonds into very small pieces.
- Make a fine paste of the remaining almonds by adding a few spoonfuls of water and grinding them.
- Mix 4 cups of water in the almond paste and keep aside.
- Melt butter.
- Add chopped onion and the remaining almonds, chopped into pieces.
- Cook for 3 or 4 minutes on slow fire till the onions are transparent.
- Remove this from fire and add sifted flour, stirring continuously.
- Add 1 cup of milk and thoroughly mix till smooth.
- Add the almond paste and water.
- Cook on a high flame till it boils.

continued...

- Add salt, pepper and sugar.
- Cook till the soup is thick.
- Stir in cream, and garnish with coriander leaves.
- Serve hot with cheese sandwiches.

BLOCK BUSTERS

You always want your child to eat to your heart's content, rather than letting him or her decide how much to eat. In fact children eat when they are hungry and until they are full, without having to be forced. Their appetites fluctuate, depending on whether they are going through a period of slow or rapid growth. It's a good idea to inculcate in them a habit of disciplined eating by observing their food habits. With a little guidance like giving them small servings to start with and then allowing for second helpings, you can do just that. These delectable hearty meals are just right for your superkids.

Ingredients for parantha
2 cups flour (*maida*)
1 cup whole wheat flour (*atta*)
1 cup corn starch (*araroot*)
1 tsp salt
½ tsp baking powder
4 or 5 tsp refined oil
a little lukewarm water for kneading the dough

Filling
2 tablespoon (6 tsp) refined oil
2 garlic flakes shopped (optional)
2 spring onions or 2 medium size onion (chopped)
2 carrots (chopped into small stripes)
1 capsicum (small bits)
100 gms mushroom or chicken (small pieces)

continued...

MALAYSIAN ENVELOPE

Serve 6 persons• Preparation time 40 minutes • Baking time 30 minutes

- Seive *maida, atta, araroot,* salt and baking powder together.
- Add oil and mix it.
- Add lukewarm water, make a smooth dough.
- Cover this with a wet napkin and keep aside for ½ an hour.

Method for filling

- Heat oil, add garlic and stir it.
- Add spring onion and sauté on a light flame (for approx. 4 minutes) till transparent.
- Add carrot, capsicum and mushroom and sauté for 3 or 4 minutes.
- Mix soya sauce, vinegar and sugar in this.
- Add shredded cabbage and salt.

continued...

1 medium size cabbage finely shredded (2 handfull)
1 tsp soya sauce
1 tsp vinegar
1 tsp salt,
½ tsp sugar

- Cool at room temperature.
- Make 8 medium size balls from the dough prepared earlier.
- Roll each ball into thin *chapati.*
- Place the filling in the centre in square shape.
- Now fold from 2 sides opposite each other overlapping each other.
- Press it and bind it.
- Similarly, fold from other 2 sides and press it till it binds.
- It resembles a square packet.
- Press the edges.
- Heat girdle (*tava*) or flat fry pan and grease it.
- Cook lightly from both sides.
- Now pour little oil from all the sides and cook till nicely golden brown from both the sides.
- Serve hot with tomato ketchup or garlic chilli sauce.

CABBAGE PARCELS

Serve 6 persons • Preparation Time 20 minute • Cooking time 20 minutes

Ingredients

6 blanched cabbage leaves
2 boiled and finely chopped potatoes
1 cup boiled peas
1 cup boiled rice (long grain)
1 diced carrot
1 finely chopped onion
½ cup cornflakes
2 tsp butter
salt to taste
¼ black pepper powder
1 tsp grated ginger
2 tsp lemon juice
½ tsp sugar
flour (*maida*) for coating
oil for shallow frying

- Boil water along with ½ tsp salt.
- Place full cabbage leaves in this water and boil for 1 minute.
- Remove from fire and let them stand for 4 or 5 minutes. Drain them.
- Melt butter, add ginger and onions and sauté for 2 minutes.
- Add sugar, stirring regularly.
- Mix potatoes, peas, boiled rice, carrot and add salt to taste.
- Remove from fire and add lemon juice and cornflakes.
- Divide it in 6 portions.
- Now remove the hard part of each blanched cabbage leaf.
- Spread one portion of the prepared filling on the leaf.

continued...

- Fold into a square parcel by folding twice.
- Coat the cabbage with flour or *maida* and dust the extra off. Repeat this with all the six leaves.
- Shallow fry the cabbage parcels in hot oil till crisp and nicely golden brown.
- Serve plain or with mint chutney mixed in curd.

<u>Try This Variation</u>

Instead of potatoes, boiled and shredded chicken can be used for filling.

PINEAPPLE AND MACARONI SALAD

Ingredients for salad
4 finely chopped pineapple slices (fresh or tinned)
1 packet boiled macaroni (short pieces)
chopped mint leaves
few cherries (fresh or tinned)

Ingredients for dressing
1 cup hung curd
½ cup chilled cream
1 tsp salt
¼ tsp pepper
5 tsp pineapple syrup (tinned)

Serve 4 persons• Preparation time 30 minutes

- Prepare the salad dressing by mixing hung curd, cream, salt, pepper and syrup.
- Beat well till smooth and keep aside.
- In a separate bowl, mix boiled macaroni, bits of pineapple slices, chopped mint leaves and cherries.
- Add the dressing and mix well.
- Garnish with lettuce leaves and bits of carrot.
- Serve chilled.

How to make Hung Curd

Tie 2½ cups of curd in muslin cloth for 1½ hours so that extra water gets separated.

DUCKLING SALAD

Serve 4 persons• Preparation time 30 minutes

Ingredients for ducklings
4 hard-boiled eggs
salt to taste
¼ tsp white pepper (optional)
1 boiled and grated potato
4 tsp grated carrot
1 grated cheese cube
½ cup finely shredded cabbage
1 tsp lemon juice
1 tsp cream or top layer of milk (*malai*)
1 small piece of carrot
few peppercorns

Ingredients for salad
1 small finely shredded cabbage
1 big thickly grated carrot
salt to taste (½ tsp)
¼ tsp white pepper
3 tsp lemon juice
½ tsp sugar
2 or 3 tsp tomato ketchup

- Shell the eggs and cut into half lengthwise.
- Separate the yolks and keep them aside.
- Mix together grated potatoes, carrot, cheese, shredded cabbage, salt, pepper, lemon juice and cream till smooth.
- Mix mashed egg yolks into the mixture.
- Fill the egg whites cases with the prepared mixture, leaving the narrow side uncovered.
- Press the filling so that it does not come out. Make the beak with a small thin triangle of a piece of carrot, and eyes with peppercorn.
- In a separate bowl add salt, pepper, sugar and lemon juice to the cabbage.
- Arrange this in a dish and garnish with grated carrot.
- Sprinkle tomato ketchup.
- Arrange ducklings all around it and one duckling (Mother Duck) in the centre.
- Serve this salad with toasted bread and butter.

YOGHURT AND FRUIT SALAD

Serve 5 persons• Preparation time 20 minutes

Ingredients
1 cup hung curd (yoghurt)
6 tsp cream (optional)
2/3 tsp salt
1 tsp castor sugar or 2 tsp honey
1/3 tsp powdered white or black pepper
½ tsp roasted and ground cumin powder (*jeera*)
chopped coriander leaves
1 big apple chopped into small cubes
1 big or 2 small cut and deseeded oranges
1 cup grapes
2 custard apples (*chikoo*) with skin removed and cut into cubes
4 or 5 strawberries (optional)
10 to 12 cherries
2 pineapple slices chopped
1 cup diced papaya

- Mix hung curd (as explained earlier), salt, pepper, cumin seeds and castor sugar.
- Beat till smooth.
- Add cream, mix well and keep aside.
- In a bowl mix all the fruits and the yoghurt dressing. Mix thoroughly.
- Garnish with coriander leaves or chopped mint leaves.
- Decorate with carrot and cucumber slices.

Try This Variation

Instead of cream, fresh *malai,* which is lightly beaten, can be used.

MAXI-BEAN SALAD

Serve 6 persons • Preparation time 30 minutes

Ingredients for salad
1 cup boiled kidney beans (*rajma*)
100 gms boiled French beans
1 cup shredded cabbage
1 thickly grated carrot
100 gms spiral pasta or any small-shaped boiled pasta
1 boiled potato diced into small cubes
1 thinly sliced capsicum
1 chopped spring onion
1 grated cheese cube
1 deseeded and chopped orange

Ingredients for dressing
6 tsp olive oil or refined oil
1 tsp salt
¼ tsp pepper
4 tsp fresh lemon juice
1 tsp sugar
¼ tsp oregano
6 tsp cream
2 tsp coriander leaves

- Mix olive oil, salt, pepper, sugar, oregano, lemon juice, cream and coriander leaves. Shake well or blend it.
- Keep this aside.
- In a separate bowl mix together the kidney beans, French beans, shredded cabbage, carrot, boiled pasta, potato, capsicum and spring onion.
- Add the salad dressing and thoroughly mix.
- Grate cheese on top and garnish with a few cherries and small orange pieces.

Ingredients for boats
4 medium-size boiled potatoes
¼ tsp salt
¼ tsp red chilli powder
¼ tsp turmeric powder (*haldi*)
2 tsp lemon juice
¼ tsp garlic paste
2 or 3 tsp refined oil
a little flour (*maida*) for coating
oil for frying

Ingredients for filling
1 cup cottage cheese (*paneer*)
1 finely chopped small onion
1 or 2 finely chopped green chillies chopped coriander leaves
1 tsp grated ginger
½ tsp salt
½ tsp roasted cumin seeds

continued...

POTATO BOATS

Serve 4 persons• Preparation time 15 minutes • Baking time 5 minutes

- Peel the boiled potatoes and cut them lengthwise.
- Scoop out the inner portion smoothly, taking care that the potatoes do not break.
- Mix salt, red chilli powder, turmeric powder, garlic, lemon juice and refined oil.
- Rub this mixture on the potato cases (inside and outside).
- Then coat with *maida.*
- Fry in hot oil till nicely golden brown.
- Keep aside.

(If you don't want to fry them then do not coat with *maida* but bake in pre-heated oven at 220°C for 10 minutes).

FILLING

- Mix *paneer*, onion, green chillies, coriander leaves, ginger,

continued...

(ground *jeera*)
a few chopped nuts and raisins
2 or 3 tsp cream
bread crumbs as required

salt, cumin seeds, nuts and raisins and cream the mixture till smooth.

- Fill this mixture firmly in each potato case and sprinkle bread crumbs on top.
- Bake in pre-heated oven at 200°C for 5 minutes.
- Arrange one thin triangular piece of carrot on each of the stuffed potatoes so that they appear like boats.
- Serve on a cabbage bed or on lettuce leaves.

Ingredients
1 mini pizza
4 tsp pizza sauce
4 tsp mozzarella cheese (pizza cheese)
2 tomato slices
a few boiled peas
1 or 2 eggplant slices
1 round slice of tomato (to make the lips)
2 slices of baby courgelt (Zucchini)
25 gms boiled noodles
1 tsp oil
a pinch of salt
1 red chilli (or tomato slice)

FUNNY-FACE PIZZA

Preparation time 7 minutes • Baking time 8 minutes

- Spread the pizza sauce on the mini pizza base and cover it with grated mozzarella cheese.
- Arrange two small tomato slices for eyes and put boiled peas in the centre of each slice.
- Make eyebrows with a thin slice of aubergine (eggplant).
- Make ears with a halved courgett slice.
- Make lips with a round slice of tomato or with red chilli.
- Sprinkle a little olive oil or melted butter on the pizza.
- Bake in a pre-heated oven at 200°C for eight to ten minutes till the edges are crisp.
- Arrange in a serving dish.
- Sauté boiled noodles in 1 tsp oil with a pinch of salt for half a minute.

continued...

Ingredients

½ kg chopped and blended tomatoes
2 tsp butter
1 finely chopped onion
½ tsp grated garlic
½ tsp grated ginger
½ tsp red chilli powder
2 or 3 cloves
1 stick of cinnamon
2 or 3 basil leaves (*tulsi*)
½ tsp salt
½ tsp sugar

- Arrange the noodles on the upper side of the pizza for the hair.
- Put small pieces of tomato or red chillies as hairpins.
- Serve immediately.

How to make Pizza Sauce

- Melt butter, add garlic, ginger and onion.
- Cook for three or four minutes on a high flame.
- Add cloves, cinnamon and basil leaves.
- Stir and add tomato puree, salt and sugar and cook for 7 to 8 minutes on high flame, till the mixture is thick.
- Remove from fire. Cool and blend it.
- You can store the sauce for a week in the refrigerator.

KING CASSEROLE

Serve 6 person • Preparation time 30 minutes • Cooking time 15 minutes

Ingredients

2 cup boiled kidney beans (*rajma*)
4 tsp butter or olive oil
½ tsp crushed garlic
1 tsp grated ginger
1 finely chopped onion
½ tsp red chilli powder
½ tsp roasted cumin seeds (*jeera*)
½ cup tomato paste
salt to taste
2 or 3 chopped basil (*tulsi*)leaves
¼ tsp oregano
1 cup boiled Penne pasta
a few chopped coriander leaves
5 tsp cream

- Melt butter.
- Add garlic and ginger and stir.
- Add chopped onions and cook till tender and transparent.
- Mix red chilli powder, roasted cumin seeds, tomato paste, basil leaves and boiled *rajma* (kidney beans).
- Cook for 3 or 4 minutes.
- Add a cup of water and salt to taste and cook till this boils.
- Add boiled Penne pasta and oregano.
- Simmer for 2 minutes.
- Pour cream and stir.
- Garnish with coriander leaves.
- Serve with roasted garlic bread and butter.

Try This Variation

- Spread the cooked kidney beans on *kulchas.*
- Grate cheese on the top and bake in a pre-heated oven at 200 C for 8 minutes, till crisp.

Funny Face Pizza ➤

Overleaf Choconut Delight

Ingredients

2 cups finely chopped French beans
1 spring onion chopped with the crisp green part
4 tsp butter
2 crushed garlic cloves
4 or 5 crushed cardamoms
salt to taste
¼ tsp pepper
1 tsp beaten curd
1 cup thick coconut milk
½ tsp cumin seeds (ground *jeera*)
chopped coriander leaves
2 tsp grated carrot

SUPER-DUPER CURRY

Serve 4 persons • Preparation time 7 minutes • Cooking time 15 minutes

- Boil beans with 1cup water and a ¼ tsp salt till almost tender.
- Pass through a sieve and reserve the water.
- Melt butter, add cardamoms and garlic to it.
- Stir and add onions and cook for 2 minutes.
- Add beans and cook for 2 more minutes.
- Add curd, salt and pepper and stir.
- Add reserved water and cook till the beans are dry.
- Add coconut milk and cook till the gravy is thick.
- Garnish with coriander leaves and grated carrot.
- Serve with *alu ka parantha* or plain *parantha* or yellow rice.

FRONTIER PANEER

Make 10 pieces • Preparation time 15 minutes • Cooking time 6 minutes

Ingredients
400 gms *paneer*
2 grated cheese cubes
1 tsp chopped onion
chopped coriander leaves
1 tsp grated ginger
1 crushed garlic clove
few chopped nuts
few raisins (25)
¼ tsp salt
¼ tsp pepper
2 tsp cream or *malai* (boiled milk's top layer)
½ cup *maida* batter
bread crumbs for coating
oil for shallow frying

- Cut *paneer* into pieces 2" by 2" square and 1" thick.
- Make slits in the centre of each and keep aside.
- In a separate bowl mix cheese, onion, coriander leaves, ginger, garlic, nuts, raisins, cream and salt and stir well till smooth.
- Fill this mixture in the *paneer* (slit) and press it.
- Similarly fill all the *paneer* pieces and keep aside.
- In a separate bowl make *maida* batter by mixing 6 tsp *maida* with milk, salt and pepper (like *pakora* batter) .
- Dip each *paneer* square into *maida* batter and fry in hot oil till lightly golden brown.
- Serve this on a bed of lettuce leaves with Thousand Island dip or any dip of your choice.

PENNE PASTA

Ingredients
200 gms boiled penne pasta
2 tbsp olive oil
½ tsp salt
½ tsp pepper
½ tsp oregano
2 tsp vinegar
1 tsp castor sugar
1 chopped spring onion or white onion
50 gms grated cheese
2 red bell pepper or green cut into small strips
2 tomatoes (skinned)
1 tsp butter
a pinch each of salt, sugar and pepper

Serve 4 person • Preparation time 20 minutes • Cooking time 12 minutes

- Mix vinegar, salt, pepper, sugar, oregano and olive oil.
- Add spring onion and penne pasta.
- Cook together for 4 or 5 minutes and keep aside.
- In a separate pan melt butter.
- Add strips of pepper and cook for 3 or 4 minutes.
- Add salt, pepper, and sugar and mix.
- Then mix in the tomato.
- Now arrange cooked hot pasta in a serving dish.
- Add cooked pepper and tomato mixture on it and then grate cheese right on the top.
- Serve it as it is or bake for 5 minutes before serving with toasted garlic bread and butter.

continued ....

How To Boil Pasta

- Boil water with ½ tsp salt and ½ tsp oil.
- Cook for 7 or 8 minutes on a high flame.
- Remove from fire and leave in water for 4 minutes.
- Pass through a sieve first and then through fresh water.
- While cooking, if it becomes sticky, rinse it again.

Ingredients

1 packet (200 gms.) of boiled noodles
4 tsp refined oil
2 crushed garlic cloves
1 chopped spring onion
¼ tsp red chilli powder
½ tsp soya sauce
1 tsp vinegar
4 tsp tomato ketchup
1 tsp salt
2 pineapple slices cut into small bits
1 cup finely chopped spinach leaves
1 capsicum chopped into small bits

PINAPPLE AND SPINACH NOODLES

Serve 4 person • Preparation time 8 minutes • Cooking time 8 minutes

- Heat oil, add garlic and chopped onion.
- Cook for 2 minutes.
- Add pineapple, spinach and capsicum and cook for a minute.
- Mix red chilli powder, soya sauce, vinegar and tomato ketchup to taste. Stir it, and add boiled noodles.
- Cook this for 2 or 3 minutes and serve hot to with garlic sauce.

FETTUCINI IN TOMATO SAUCE

Serve 6 persons • Preparation time 20 minutes • Cooking time 15 minutes • Baking time 10 minutes

Ingredients

200 gms fettucini, i.e. boiled ribbon pasta
6 tsp olive oil or 4 tsp butter
½ tsp garlic paste
½ tsp salt and ½ tsp white or black pepper
1 cup Italian tomato sauce
2 tsp olive oil or butter
2 thin, round slices of baby courgetts (Zucchini)
1 capsicum cut into small strips
2 chopped spring onion
1 boiled potato cut into small cubes
2 chopped green chillies
½ tsp oregano
½ tsp salt
½ tsp sugar
½ cup cream
2 cheese cubes or 50 gms pizza cheese

- Heat olive oil, add garlic and stir.
- Add boiled pasta, salt and pepper. Cook for 3 or 4 minutes. Keep aside.
- In a separate pan heat oil or melt butter.
- Add onions and cook for 4 minutes till transparent and mix sliced baby courgettes, capsicum, potato cubes and green chillies.
- Cook for 3 or 4 minutes.
- Add salt, pepper, and oregano and cook for a minute.
- Mix Italian tomato sauce.
- Now arrange pasta in oven compatible serving dish.
- Pour the above mixture in the centre.
- Pour cream and grated cheese on it.
- Bake in a pre-heated oven at 200°C for 10 minutes till the cheese is golden brown. Serve hot.

continued...

Ingredients

2 tsp butter
½ tsp grated garlic
½ tsp grated ginger
2 cloves
a pinch of cinnamon powder
6 or 7 finely chopped medium-size tomatoes
½ tsp salt
½ tsp sugar

How to make Italian Tomato Sauce:

- Melt butter.
- Add ginger, garlic, and clove.
- Cook for a minute.
- Add chopped tomatoes, cinnamon, salt and sugar.
- Cook for 5 minutes on high flame.
- Cool and churn it.

OODLE-SMOODLE FRITTERS

Serve 6 persons • Preparation time 15 minutes • Cooking time 10 minutes

Ingredients

1 packet of boiled Maggie noodles or any chow noodles
½ tsp salt
1 cup boiled assorted vegetables (carrot, beans, peas and spinach)
¼ tsp white pepper
2 tsp tomato ketchup
6 tsp corn flour
1 crushed garlic clove
a pinch of salt and pepper
1 lightly beaten egg
oil for frying

- Break noodles into small pieces and boil for 2 minutes.
- Pass through a sieve and cool this.
- Mix salt, pepper and vegetables.
- Add tomato ketchup and thoroughly mix it.
- Now divide the mixture into 10 equal portions and press into round shapes.
- Make batter with cornflour, garlic, salt, pepper and beaten egg.
- Now dip each round portion of noodles in cornflour batter till coated thoroughly.
- Fry in hot oil till lightly golden brown.
- Serve hot with garlic chilli sauce.
- For eggless batter add a little milk, instead of the egg.

SWEET TREATS & SHAKES

"But Mommy, I hate milk!" This is the constant refrain of your child which you hate to hear, aware as you are that milk and dairy products are essential for your child's health. It is these items which provide the requisite calcium and protein necessary for making strong bones and encouraging healthy growth. Relax, now no more coaxing or cajoling is required! With the amazing recipes for shakes and ice-creams given inside, you can give your child all the essential nutrients plus the taste!

Ingredients for cake
2/3 cup castor sugar
1 cup flour (*maida*)
1 tsp baking powder
2 tsp cocoa powder
½ tsp soda bi-carb
1 finely grated apple
2 eggs(lightly beaten)
¾ cup chopped nuts
1 cup grated carrot
½ cup oil

Ingredients for cream frosting
½ cup chilled cream
½ cup desicated coconut
1 cup icing sugar
2 drops vanilla essence (optional)

CARROT CAKE

Serve 6 persons • Preparation time 40 minutes • Baking time 30 minutes

- Pre-heat the oven at 180°C for 10 minutes.
- Sift the flour, castor sugar, baking powder, cocoa powder and soda together.
- Add the lightly beaten eggs, grated carrot, grated apple And oil. Mix thoroughly with a wooden spatula.
- Line the cake mould with greased brown paper and pour the mixture into it.
- Bake at 180°C for 35 minutes.
- Insert a dry knife into the cake; if it comes out clean the cake is ready.
- Leave the cake to cool.
- Serve it plain or with cream frosting.

continued...

CREAM FROSTING

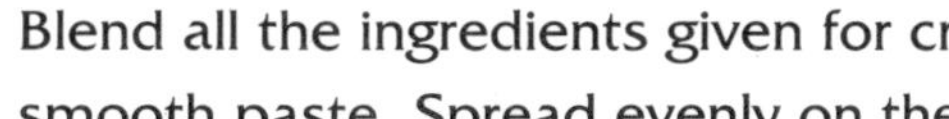

Blend all the ingredients given for cream frosting into a smooth paste. Spread evenly on the top and sides of the cake.

CHOCONUT DELIGHT

Serve 6 persons • Cooking time 15 minutes

Ingredients
3 cups milk
2/3 cup sugar
4 tsp cornflour
½ cup cold milk
2 tsp cocoa powder
½ tsp vanilla essence
½ cup chilled cream
½ cup chopped walnuts
1 medium-size dairy-milk chocolate
a few cherries

- Boil the milk and add the sugar. Cook for 3 minutes.
- Stir cornflour and 2 tsp cocoa powder in ½ cup cold milk till smooth.
- Pour the cocoa mixture in the boiled milk and cook on slow fire till it turns thick.
- Cool it and add vanilla essence.
- Beat the cream till it is thick like custard and mix it in the cocoa mixture.
- Add the walnuts and chopped chocolate pieces.
- Pour this into a serving bowl, chill it garnish with cream and cherries.

Try This Variation

You can use 1 tsp coffee and ½ tsp cocoa instead of cocoa powder to make Coffee delight.

Various Shakes ➤

Overleaf Mango Delight

Ingredients
6 oranges
2/3 cup sugar
1 tsp lemon juice
2 tsp gelatine
½ cup hot water for dissolving gelatine
2 drops red colour (edible)
2 drops green colour
2/3 cup cream (150 gms)
3 tsp castor sugar

ORANGE BASKET PUDDING

Serve 6 persons• Preparation time 20 minutes • Cooking time 5 minutes • Chilling time 50 minutes

- With a sharp knife carve out a semi-circular basket with a handle on each orange in such a manner that the lower half remains untouched while on the upper half 2 semi circles leaving 2½"-3" wide strip in the middle are carved out. This strip becomes the handle of the basket.
- Scoop out the pulp from the lower half of the basket and also from whatever remains in the handle or the top portion.
- Clean the orange basket and rinse it with cold water.
- Squeeze out the juice from the extracted pulp and pass it through a sieve.
- Add sugar and cook this juice on slow fire till the sugar dissolves.

continued...

- Soak gelatine in hot water and mix it into the orange mixture by stirring it for a minute.
- Remove it from fire and cool it.
- In half the portion, add red colour and in the other half add green.
- Put each portion in separate flat bowls and keep them in the freezer to set.
- Unmould both the portions and cut into small cubes.
- Fill up orange basket with the green and red cubes.
- Beat cream with castor sugar till soft peaks are formed.
- Make florets with cream over the cubes in the basket and garnish with cherries and mint leaves.
- Serve chilled.

MAGIC BREAD COOKIES

Make 12 cookies • Preparation time 30 minutes • Baking time 15 minutes

Ingredients
6 bread slices
butter as desired
3 tsp jam or marmalade
½ cup condensed milk (Milkmaid)
2 tsp cocoa powder
½ tsp vanilla essence
5 tsp milk
½ cup desicated coconut
a few nuts and cherries

- Remove the hard crust of bread slices and butter them lightly.
- Spread 1 tsp jam thinly on each slice and make sandwiches.
- Cut jam sandwiches with any fancy cutter or else cut them into four square pieces.
- Keep aside.
- Mix condensed milk, cocoa powder, vanilla essence and milk till smooth.
- Pre-heat oven at 200°C for 10 minutes and arrange greased foil on the baking tray.
- Dip each piece of bread in the chocolate mixture till thoroughly coated.

continued...

- Spread desicated coconut in a dish and coat the cookies.
- Place these on the baking tray.
- Repeat this procedure with all the bread slices and arrange them on the baking tray.
- Arrange 1 almond or walnut and 1 cherry on each cookie .
- Bake the cookie in the pre-heated oven for 15 minutes.
- Allow it to cool for 3 or 4 minutes. With the help of a butter knife or spatula remove the cookies.
- Place in a serving dish or in pastry cases before serving.

MANGO DELIGHT

Serve 6 persons • Preparation time 30 minutes • Chilling time 2 hrs • Cooking time 6 minutes

Ingredients
1 ½ cup fresh or tinned mango juice
2/3 cup sugar
½ tsp mango essence
2 tsp lemon juice
2 cups chilled cream
3 medium-size mangoes, chopped into small pieces
2 tsp gelatine
½ cup hot water for dissolving gelatine

- Dissolve gelatine in 1/2 cup hot water, stirring continuously.
- Heat mango juice and sugar in a pan till the sugar dissolves.
- Remove from fire and mix gelatine in it for 2 minutes.
- Now cool it on ice and water and stir continuously till thick and syrupy.
- Add mango essence and lemon juice to this mixture.
- Beat chilled cream till thick and add to the mango juice mixture.
- Stir on iced water till it resembles custard.
- Add chopped mango pieces to this mixture serving bowl.
- Keep it in the freezer for nearly 2 hours till it sets.
- Garnish with cherries and pieces of mango.

continued...

<u>Precautions</u>

To avoid crystal formation, do not keep this dish in the freezing chamber for a very long time. In case you want to store it for longer, place it in the normal refrigerator and put it back in the freezer only ½ an hour before serving.

CHOCOLATE BREAD PUDDING

Serve 6 persons • Preparation time 15 minutes • Baking time 35 minutes

Ingredients
12 bread slices
2 ½ cups hot milk
1 cup castor sugar
4 tsp cocoa powder
1 tsp baking powder
½ tsp vanilla essence
2 tsp honey (optional)
a few walnuts and raisins

- Remove the hard crust from the bread slices.
- Crumble the bread into small bits or else churn it in a dry grinder.
- Add castor sugar, baking powder and cocoa powder.
- Mix thoroughly.
- Pour hot milk, honey and vanilla essence and mix well.
- Keep the mixture aside for 5 minutes till soft.
- Mix and mash the mixture with metal spoon.
- Mix walnuts and raisins.
- Pre-heat oven at 200°C 10 for minutes.
- Line the mould with greased aluminium foil and pour the mixture into the mould.
- Bake the mixture at 200°C for 15 minutes. Then reduce the temperature to 180°C and again bake for 20 minutes till set.

continued...

- After 5 minutes loosen the edges and unmould it. Spread walnuts or jam on top.
- Serve it plain or with whipped cream or vanilla ice-cream and roasted nuts.

Ingredients

1 cup almonds (soaked and peeled)
4 cups of milk
1 cup sugar
4 or 5 crushed cardamoms or 1/4th tsp cardomom powder
1/4th tsp saffron (*kesar*)
1/3th cup rice (soaked for 1 hour) and grind it to fine paste by adding little water
½ cup milk for mixing rice paste
few flaked almonds, raisins and cherries
2 tsp *kewra jal* or *gulab jal*

BADAM KHEER

Serve 6 persons • Preparation time 10 minutes • Cooking time 20 minutes

- Make a fine paste of almonds in small grinder by adding a few spoons of milk till smooth.
- Keep aside.
- Boil milk along with crushed cardamoms and *kesar*.
- When it starts boiling add sugar and almond paste and thoroughly mix it.
- Cook it on medium flame for 4 or 5 minutes.
- Now mix rice paste with ½ cup cold milk till smooth and pour it into *badam* mixture.
- Cook it on slow fire till thick like custard.
- Remove from fire and cool it.
- Add *kewra* jal.
- Garnish with nuts, raisins and cherries.

You can serve *Badam Kheer* warm as well as cold.

Ingredients
8 tsp cocoa powder
1 cup castor sugar
½ cup chilled cream
½ tsp vanilla essence
½ cup roasted and chopped walnuts
1/3 cup roasted cashewnuts
a few chopped cherries
crushed ice as desired
4 cup milk

CHOCOLATE NUT SHAKE

Serve 4 persons • Preparation time 6 minutes

- Blend together cocoa, castor sugar, crushed ice and half cup of milk till smooth.
- Add cream and churn it in a mixer.
- Now add the rest of the milk and churn again fora minute.
- Pour the shake in glasses.
- Garnish with 1 tsp cream, roasted nuts and chopped cherries.